Launch Your Signature Course in 5 Days:
A Step-by-Step Guide for Entrepreneurs

Disclaimer

The information and recipes contained in this book are based upon the research and the personal experiences of the author. It's for entertainment purposes only. It is not meant to replace any advice from a health care professional. This book is meant to compliment. The reader is encouraged to use good judgement when applying the information contained and to seek advice from a qualified professional if, and as needed. Professionals should be consulted as needed prior to undertaking any of the actions endorsed herein.

Every attempt has been made to provide accurate, up to date and reliable information. No warranties of any kind are expressed or implied. Readers acknowledge that the author is not engaging in the rendering of legal, financial, medical, or professional advice. By reading this, the reader agrees that under no circumstance the author is not responsible for any loss, direct or indirect, which is incurred by using this information contained within this book. Including but not limited to errors, omissions, or inaccuracies. This book is not intended as a replacement from what your health care provider has suggested. The author is not responsible for any adverse effects or consequences resulting from the use of any of

conflict of interest. This declaration is deemed fair and valid by both the American Bar association and the committee of publishers' association and is legally binding throughout the world.

By purchasing this book, you are consenting to its contents. It is important to note that the author of this book is not an expert on the topics discussed within, and any recommendations or suggestions made are for entertainment purposes only. It is recommended that professionals be consulted before taking any actions discussed in this book. This declaration has been deemed fair and valid by the American Bar Association and the Committee of Publishers' Association and is legally binding worldwide. The information contained in this book is considered truthful and accurate, and any use or misuse of the information is solely at the reader's discretion. The author cannot be held liable for any hardship or damages that may result from the reader's actions after reading this book.

A.L. Childers

All the data, research, footnotes, and references are cited in the back of the book, and it does back up all claims that have been discussed by the author. The internet is a valuable source of information, but unlike printed works, it cannot be relied upon for long-term reference. News articles may be removed from their websites, and data that you have cited may be erased, or the websites may have been terminated. This represents a challenge to authors who want to document the origin of their information.

Dear readers, it is important to take all necessary precautions before undertaking any DIY project. Always follow the instructions and be extra careful when creating your own homemade products. It is never a good idea to stretch yourself too thin. Remember that every fabric or material may react differently to suggested use. While this is a non-toxic and natural way to clean your home, it is always recommended to wear protective gloves and eyewear. Please note that although every effort has been made to provide you with the best possible information, neither the publisher nor the author is responsible for any accidents, injuries, or damage incurred because of tasks performed by readers. The author will not assume any responsibility for personal or property damage resulting from the formulas found in this book. It is important to keep in mind that this book is separate from professional services.

Authors note:

Please note that any reference or resemblance to any person or organization in this book, whether living or dead, existing, or defunct, is purely coincidental. I want to remind all readers that all rights are reserved and no part of this book or any associated ancillary materials may be reproduced or transmitted in any form by any means, electronic or mechanical, including photocopying, recording, duplicating, or by any informational storage or retrieval system, without express written permission from the author. It is important to respect the author's intellectual property and adhere to copyright laws.

A note of caution:

Prioritizing your own health and well-being is essential for a fulfilling life. I firmly believe that self-care and personal health empowerment are powerful tools, and that everyone should take the initiative to improve their own understanding. The more knowledge you have, the more control you have over your own health. However, it's important to remember that consulting with a trained medical professional is always necessary in cases of long-standing and undiagnosed symptoms. This book is not intended to replace professional medical judgment but can certainly serve as a valuable supplement to it. Stay informed and vigilant, but always remember to seek professional advice when needed. Please note that the information provided in this book is for educational and entertainment purposes only, and no warranty is given concerning the accuracy of this information. Be smart, be sensible, and prioritize your health by utilizing good common sense. Above all else, be kind and compassionate towards yourself, your body, and your mind.

An entity is different and specific to each individual or item to which it has attached itself. As to alternative forms of medicine or healing, the author of this book has yet to offer any promised outcomes. Some human issues are more profound than cleansing a new home or spiritual entity possession and removal. Therefore, you must understand that this isn't a quick fix for issues that may have gone on in your or someone else's life. Cleansing a new home or spiritual entity possession and removal is not designed as a replacement for traditional psychological and medical treatment or advice, and it is not intended to treat, diagnose, cure, or prevent any disease. There is a difference between entity removal, energy healing, deep-rooted physiological issues, and demonic possession. If you or someone you know seems to have signs of demonic activity, you should contact a priest for counsel and prayer. In addition, with the corporation and aid of a medical professional, they can help you discern if the symptoms have a more natural cause, physiological or physical. A priest can perform exorcisms if no such reasons can be clearly identified or if they seem to be occupied by a spirit. We don't need special authorization to perform deliverance prayers on a person, place, or object, but if it is an exorcism, you must have someone skilled and trained to perform it correctly.

All in all, a spiritual entity possession and entity attachment removal is not something you merely play around with. A demon will eat your lunch and pop that bag right before you.

As befitted in nature and a world that cannot be seen with human eyes, the author is protected by a binding spell of any malicious intent. Any dark or evil force may return to its source, shield my home, health, heart, and mind, as this includes all family, friends, objects, and animals of mine, as we remain free, always safe, and well indeed. You are bound to return to your source with flight; I banish thee with this holy light.

Dear Creator, please grant me your protection from those who attempt to justify evil actions as good and twist truth into lies to achieve their malicious intentions. I ask that you guard me and my loved ones against any forms of deceit and schemes against righteousness. May we be surrounded by the purest vibrations and a sphere of White Light that encompasses every corner, crack, and shelter of our dwellings. Please keep this sphere of White Light free from any negative or harmful energies, especially those of demonic origin. I also request that this sphere of White Light be expanded to cover the space that we always inhabit, ensuring our safety and well-being. Thank you for your guidance and protection.

Chapter 1: Introduction to Launching Your Signature Course

Understanding the Importance of a Signature Course

As entrepreneurs, we constantly seek ways to expand our reach, impact, and income. One of the most powerful ways to achieve this is by creating and launching a signature course. A signature course is a unique and comprehensive program that represents your expertise, knowledge, and brand. It is a powerful tool that can transform your business and catapult you to the forefront of your industry.

So, why is a signature course so important? Let's delve into the reasons and discover the immense value it can bring to your entrepreneurial journey.

First and foremost, a signature course allows you to share your expertise with a broader audience. You have spent years cultivating your skills and knowledge, and it's time to package them into a structured curriculum that can be easily consumed and applied by others. By doing so, you position yourself as an authority in your niche and attract a loyal following of eager learners.

Moreover, a signature course provides a scalable income stream. Instead of relying solely on one-on-one services or selling physical products, a course allows you to leverage your time and reach a wider audience. With proper planning and execution, your course can generate passive income, freeing up your time for other business ventures or personal pursuits.

Creating a signature course also establishes your credibility and builds trust with your audience. When you offer a comprehensive program that addresses their pain points and provides actionable solutions, you become their go-to resource. This trust translates into long-term relationships, repeat customers, and referrals to others seeking your expertise.

Additionally, a signature course positions you as a thought leader in your industry. It opens doors to speaking engagements, media opportunities, and collaborations with other industry experts. Your course becomes a powerful tool for networking and expanding your professional connections.

Finally, a signature course allows you to make a lasting impact on people's lives. By sharing your knowledge and empowering others, you become a catalyst for their success. Witnessing your students achieve their goals and transform their lives creates a sense of fulfillment and purpose that goes beyond financial rewards.

In conclusion, understanding the importance of a signature course is essential for entrepreneurs looking to take their business to the next level. It offers the opportunity to share your expertise, generate scalable income, build credibility, become a thought leader, and make a lasting impact. So, embrace the challenge and embark on the journey of planning, writing, and building your signature course. It's time to launch your course and unlock the limitless potential that awaits you.

Benefits of Launching Your Signature Course in a 5-day Challenge

Launching a signature course is an exciting endeavor for any entrepreneur. It allows you to share your expertise, impact lives, and generate income. But have you ever considered launching your signature course through a 5-day challenge? This subchapter explores the benefits of this unique approach and how it can transform your course launch.

1. Increased Engagement: A 5-day challenge creates a sense of urgency and excitement among your audience. By condensing your course content into a shorter timeframe, you encourage participants to fully immerse themselves, resulting in higher engagement levels. The daily challenges keep them motivated and eager to complete the course.

2. Faster Course Creation: The time constraint of a 5-day challenge forces you to streamline your course creation process. It pushes you to focus on the essential content and deliver it in a concise and effective manner. This accelerated timeline enables you to launch your course sooner, capitalizing on your momentum and enthusiasm.

3. Building a Community: Launching your signature course through a 5-day challenge allows you to cultivate a strong community of like-minded individuals. Participants bond through shared experiences, supporting and encouraging each other throughout the challenge. This community spirit creates a positive and motivating environment, fostering long-term connections and potential collaborations.

4. Testimonials and Social Proof: A 5-day challenge provides you with an opportunity to gather testimonials and social proof for your course. As participants experience quick wins and transformations during the challenge, they are more likely to share their positive experiences. These testimonials can be powerful marketing tools to attract future students and build credibility.

5. Immediate Revenue Generation: Unlike traditional course launches that require weeks or even months of preparation, a 5-day challenge allows you to start generating revenue immediately. By offering a limited-time enrollment window, you create a sense of urgency for participants to sign up and join the challenge. This quick influx of revenue can provide a financial boost and validate the demand for your course.

6. Preparing for Future Launches: Launching your signature course through a 5-day challenge provides valuable insights and feedback from your audience. You can gather data on what worked well, what needs improvement, and what additional content or support your students may require. This feedback will help you refine and enhance your course for future launches, maximizing its impact and profitability.

In conclusion, launching your signature course through a 5-day challenge offers numerous benefits for entrepreneurs. It increases engagement, accelerates course creation, builds a community, generates testimonials, provides immediate revenue, and prepares you for future launches. Embrace the power of a 5-day challenge and unlock the full potential of your signature course launch.

Setting Realistic Expectations for Your Course Launch

When it comes to launching your signature course, it's essential to set realistic expectations right from the start. While it's natural to be filled with enthusiasm and excitement about the potential success of your course, it's important to temper those expectations to ensure a smoother and more manageable launch process. In this subchapter, we will delve into the key factors that entrepreneurs should consider when setting realistic expectations for their course launch.

First and foremost, it's crucial to recognize that launching a course in just five days is an ambitious goal. While it is possible with proper planning and execution, it's essential to understand that this timeframe may not allow for a fully polished and comprehensive course. Instead, focus on creating a solid foundation during the launch period, with plans to refine and expand the course over time.

Another important aspect to consider is the target audience for your course. Understanding their needs, interests, and pain points will help you tailor your content to meet their expectations. However, it's important to remember that you may not be able to cater to every individual's specific needs. Instead, focus on providing value to a broader audience and offering additional support or resources for those who require more personalized attention.

Additionally, managing your own expectations is vital. Recognize that the success of your course launch may not always be measured solely by the number of participants or immediate financial gains. Instead, consider the impact you can make on the lives of your students and the long-term growth potential of your course. Remember that building a successful course takes time, and it's essential to remain patient and persistent throughout the process.

Lastly, be prepared for challenges and setbacks. Launching a course can be a complex and unpredictable journey. There may be technical issues, marketing hurdles, or unexpected obstacles along the way. By acknowledging and accepting these challenges as a part of the process, you can better navigate them and find solutions efficiently.

Setting realistic expectations for your course launch is crucial for entrepreneurs. By understanding the limitations of a five-day timeframe, catering to your target audience's broader needs, managing your own expectations, and being prepared for challenges, you can create a solid foundation for a successful course launch. Remember, this is just the beginning of your course-building journey, and with time and dedication, you can continuously refine and expand your signature course to meet the needs of your growing audience.

Chapter 2: Identifying Your Niche and Target Audience

Defining Your Niche and Finding Your Unique Selling Proposition

One of the most crucial steps in launching your signature course is defining your niche and finding your unique selling proposition (USP). As an entrepreneur, it is essential to understand that a successful course is built on a solid foundation of targeting the right audience and offering something unique that sets you apart from your competitors. In this subchapter, we will explore the process of defining your niche and uncovering your USP to ensure the success of your 5-day challenge launch.

To begin, let's dive into the concept of niche. Your niche is the specific segment of the market that you will target with your course. It is essential to narrow down your focus to a specific group of people who have a common problem or desire. By doing so, you can tailor your content and marketing efforts to meet their specific needs, making your course more appealing and effective.

Once you have identified your niche, the next step is to find your unique selling proposition. Your USP is what sets you apart from your competition and makes your course stand out in the crowded online learning space. Consider what makes your course different or better than others in the market. It could be your expertise in the subject matter, a unique teaching methodology, or even the results your students can expect to achieve. Your USP should be something that resonates with your target audience and compels them to choose your course over others.

Finding your USP requires careful research and introspection. Start by analyzing your competitors and identifying what they are offering. Look for gaps in the market or areas where you can provide a fresh perspective. Additionally, reflect on your own strengths, experiences, and expertise that make you uniquely qualified to teach your course. By combining market research with self-awareness, you can uncover your USP and use it as a cornerstone of your course's marketing strategy.

Defining your niche and finding your USP are crucial steps in launching your signature course successfully. By targeting a specific audience and offering something unique, you can position yourself as an authority in your field and attract the right students. Take the time to research your niche, analyze your competition, and reflect on your own strengths. With a well-defined niche and a compelling USP, you will be well on your way to creating and launching a successful course in just five days.

Understanding Your Target Audience's Needs and Desires

In the fast-paced world of entrepreneurship, launching a signature course can be a game-changer for your business. But before you dive into the planning, writing, and building process, it's crucial to understand your target audience's needs and desires. This subchapter will guide you through the steps necessary to truly connect with your audience, ensuring that your course is tailored to their specific wants and expectations.

To begin, it's essential to conduct extensive market research. This involves analyzing your target audience's demographics, psychographics, and pain points. By understanding who they are, what motivates them, and the challenges they face, you can tailor your course content to meet their specific needs. This research can be done through surveys, interviews, and studying industry trends to gain a holistic perspective.

Once you have a clear understanding of your target audience, the next step is to identify their desires and aspirations. What are they hoping to achieve? What are their goals and dreams? By tapping into these desires, you can create course materials that resonate deeply with your audience, providing them with the tools and knowledge they need to reach their objectives.

Additionally, it's crucial to consider the different learning styles and preferences of your target audience. Some individuals may prefer visual content, while others may prefer written or audio materials. By offering a variety of formats, you can cater to the diverse needs of your audience, ensuring that they can engage with your course in a way that suits them best.

Furthermore, engaging with your target audience through various channels, such as social media platforms or industry forums, can provide invaluable insights into their needs and desires. Engage in conversations, ask questions, and actively listen to their feedback. This will not only help you refine your course content but also build a strong rapport with your audience, fostering trust and loyalty.

Remember, understanding your target audience's needs and desires is the foundation for a successful signature course launch. By investing time and effort into researching and connecting with your audience, you can create a course that not only meets their expectations but also exceeds them. So, take the time to truly understand your audience, and watch your course become a transformative experience for both you and your students.

In a nutshell, this subchapter has emphasized the importance of understanding your target audience's needs and desires when launching your signature course. Through market research, identifying desires and aspirations, considering learning styles, and engaging with your audience, you can create a course that resonates deeply with your target audience. By doing so, you'll not only meet their expectations but also provide them with the tools and knowledge they need to achieve their goals. So, take the time to truly understand your audience, and watch your course become a transformative experience for both you and your students.

Conducting Market Research to Validate Your Course Idea

One of the key steps in launching a successful signature course is conducting thorough market research to validate your course idea. As an entrepreneur, you want to ensure that your course will resonate with your target audience and meet their specific needs. This subchapter will guide you through the process of conducting market research effectively.

Market research allows you to gain valuable insights into your target audience, their preferences, pain points, and existing solutions available in the market. By understanding your audience better, you can tailor your course content to meet their expectations and stand out from the competition.

To begin your market research, start by identifying your target audience. Who are they? What are their demographics? What are their goals and challenges? These questions will help you create a clear profile of your ideal student. Once you have a clear picture, you can then move on to conducting surveys, interviews, and analyzing online forums and social media groups where your target audience hangs out.

Surveys are a great way to collect quantitative data from a large sample size. Create a survey with questions that will help you understand your audience's needs, preferences, and pain points. Use online survey tools like Google Forms or SurveyMonkey to distribute your survey and collect responses. Analyze the data to identify common themes and patterns that will inform your course content.

Interviews are another powerful tool for gathering qualitative data. Reach out to individuals who fit your target audience profile and conduct one-on-one interviews. Ask open-ended questions to encourage detailed responses and gain deeper insights into their needs and challenges. The information gathered through interviews can help you refine your course content and make it more relevant to your audience.

Finally, analyze online forums and social media groups related to your niche. These platforms are gold mines of information, where people openly discuss their problems and seek solutions. Pay attention to the questions, comments, and discussions happening in these communities. Identify recurring themes and topics that will help you create content that directly addresses your audience's pain points.

By conducting comprehensive market research, you will gain a deep understanding of your target audience and their needs. This knowledge will serve as a solid foundation for creating a signature course that resonates with your audience and sets you apart from the competition. So, take the time to validate your course idea through market research, and you'll be well on your way to launching a successful course.

Chapter 3: Planning Your Signature Course

Determining Your Course Goals and Objectives

In order to successfully launch your signature course, it is crucial to determine your course goals and objectives right from the start. This subchapter will guide you through the process of clarifying your vision and setting clear objectives, ensuring that your course is targeted and effective for your audience of entrepreneurs.

The first step in determining your course goals is to define your overall vision. What do you want to achieve with your course? What problem are you solving for your audience? Take some time to brainstorm and write down your ultimate goals and aspirations for your course. This will serve as your guiding light throughout the course creation process.

Once you have a clear vision, it's time to set specific course objectives. These objectives should be measurable and aligned with your overall vision. They will serve as the roadmap for your course, helping you stay focused and on track. Consider what knowledge and skills your audience should gain from your course, and how you can deliver the most value to them.

Another important aspect to consider when determining your course goals and objectives is your target audience. Who are the entrepreneurs you want to reach? What are their pain points, needs, and desires? By understanding your target audience, you can tailor your course content and objectives to meet their specific needs, ensuring that it resonates with them and provides tangible results.

Also it is essential to establish realistic and achievable goals. While it's great to aim high, setting unattainable goals can lead to frustration and disappointment. Break down your overall objectives into smaller, manageable milestones. By doing so, you can track your progress and celebrate your achievements along the way.

Throughout this subchapter, we will explore various techniques and strategies to help you determine your course goals and objectives effectively. From conducting market research to identifying your unique selling proposition, you will gain valuable insights into how to plan, write, and build your signature course in a 5-day challenge launch.

Remember, the success of your course lies in your ability to clearly define your course goals and objectives. By taking the time to understand your vision, audience, and setting realistic milestones, you are one step closer to creating a course that resonates with entrepreneurs and delivers exceptional value. So, let's dive in and get started on your journey to launching your signature course!

Outlining Your Course Content and Structure

In the exciting journey of launching your signature course, one crucial step is outlining your course content and structure. This subchapter will guide you through the process of planning, writing, and building your course in just five days. By the end of this chapter, you will have a clear roadmap to create a powerful and impactful course that resonates with your audience.

Before diving into the specifics, it is essential to understand the significance of a well-structured course. Your course's structure determines how your content flows, how your students learn, and ultimately impacts their success. A solid structure ensures that your course is easy to follow, engaging, and delivers the desired outcomes.

To begin outlining your course, start by defining your learning objectives. What do you want your students to achieve by the end of the course? Break down these objectives into specific modules or lessons that build upon each other. This step will help you create a logical progression of content and ensure that your students grasp the concepts effectively.

Next, consider the different types of content you will include in your course. Will you have video lessons, written materials, quizzes, or interactive exercises? Determine the best format for each topic, keeping in mind your target audience's preferences and learning styles. Variety is key to keeping your students engaged and motivated throughout the course.

Once you have identified the content types, focus on creating compelling and informative lessons within each module. Each lesson should have a clear structure, including an introduction, learning objectives, main content, and a summary or conclusion. Break down complex concepts into digestible chunks and provide examples and real-life applications to illustrate your points.

While outlining your course, consider incorporating interactive elements to enhance student engagement. This could include discussion forums, group activities, case studies, or even live Q&A sessions. By encouraging student interaction, you foster a sense of community and increase the overall learning experience.

Lastly, revisit your course outline and ensure that it aligns with your target audience's needs and expectations. Seek feedback from trusted individuals who fit your target audience profile to validate your course structure and content choices.

In general, outlining your course content and structure is a crucial step to launching a successful signature course. By clearly defining your learning objectives, utilizing various content formats, creating engaging lessons, and incorporating interactive elements, you will create a course that captivates your audience and delivers results. So, grab a pen and paper, and let's start outlining your course content and structure!

Creating Engaging Lesson Plans and Modules

In the world of online education, creating engaging lesson plans and modules is crucial to the success of your signature course. As an entrepreneur, you have the opportunity to share your expertise and knowledge with others, but it is essential to present your content in a way that captivates and motivates your audience. This subchapter will guide you through the process of designing lesson plans and modules that are not only informative but also engaging, ensuring the success of your 5-day challenge launch.

When creating lesson plans, it is important to start by defining clear objectives for each module. What do you want your students to achieve after completing this particular lesson? By clearly outlining your goals, you can structure your content accordingly, ensuring that each lesson is focused and concise. Additionally, consider incorporating a variety of instructional strategies to cater to different learning styles. This could include videos, interactive quizzes, case studies, or hands-on exercises.

To further engage your audience, make sure your lessons are structured in a logical and easy-to-follow manner. Begin with an attention-grabbing introduction that sets the stage for what's to come, followed by the main content and a summary or key takeaways at the end. Break down complex concepts into smaller, digestible chunks, and use visual aids such as images, charts, or infographics to enhance understanding.

Another key aspect of creating engaging lesson plans is to encourage active participation from your students. Incorporate opportunities for discussion, reflection, and application of the concepts learned. This could be done through interactive online forums, group activities, or even one-on-one coaching sessions. By fostering a sense of community and interaction, you not only keep your students engaged but also provide them with a platform to share their thoughts and learn from each other.

In fine, regularly assess and evaluate your lesson plans and modules. Seek feedback from your students and make adjustments as necessary. This iterative process will help you continually improve and refine your content, ensuring that your signature course remains relevant and effective.

To conclude, creating engaging lesson plans and modules is a crucial step in the success of your signature course. By defining clear objectives, using a variety of instructional strategies, structuring your content logically, encouraging active participation, and regularly assessing and evaluating your materials, you can ensure that your course is informative, captivating, and beneficial for your students.

Chapter 4: Writing Compelling Course Content

Crafting a Powerful Course Introduction

The course introduction is the first impression your students will have of your signature course. It sets the tone for the entire learning experience and plays a crucial role in capturing your audience's attention from the start. A well-crafted introduction can make or break the success of your course, so it's essential to get it right. In this subchapter, we will explore the key elements of a powerful course introduction and guide you through the process of creating one that leaves a lasting impact on your students.

First and foremost, a powerful course introduction needs to grab your audience's attention. Start with a compelling hook that immediately sparks curiosity and makes them want to know more. This could be a thought-provoking question, a surprising statistic, or a relatable story that resonates with your target audience. By engaging them right from the start, you will ignite their interest and motivate them to continue with the course.

Next, clearly outline the purpose and objectives of your signature course. Explain what problem your course solves and how it will benefit your students. This will help them understand the value they will gain from participating and keep them motivated throughout the learning journey.

Additionally, it's crucial to establish your credibility as an expert in your niche. Share your background, qualifications, and personal experiences that make you uniquely qualified to teach the course. This builds trust and reassures your students that they are learning from someone who knows what they're talking about.

To create a sense of community and foster engagement, introduce the structure of the course and any interactive elements you have incorporated. Let your students know that they are not alone in their learning journey and that they can expect a supportive and interactive environment. This will encourage them to actively participate and make the most out of the course.

Lastly, end your course introduction with a clear call to action. Outline the next steps for your students, whether it's accessing the course materials, joining a discussion group, or completing a pre-course survey. By providing a clear roadmap, you guide your students towards success and show them that you are committed to their learning experience.

Crafting a powerful course introduction is a crucial step in launching your signature course. It sets the tone, engages your audience, and motivates them to continue with the course. By incorporating the key elements discussed in this subchapter, you will create an introduction that captivates your audience and sets the stage for a successful learning experience.

Developing High-Quality Lesson Materials

Creating engaging and valuable lesson materials is a crucial aspect of building a successful signature course. As an entrepreneur venturing into the world of online education, it is essential to understand the significance of high-quality lesson materials in attracting and retaining students. In this subchapter, we will explore effective strategies and tips to develop top-notch lesson materials that will leave a lasting impact on your audience.

First and foremost, it is important to conduct thorough research on your course topic. Understanding your target audience's needs and preferences will allow you to tailor your lesson materials accordingly. By providing relevant and up-to-date information, you can establish yourself as an expert in your niche and build trust with your students.

When it comes to planning your lesson materials, it is crucial to have a clear structure and organization. Start by outlining the main topics and subtopics you wish to cover in your course. Break down each lesson into smaller sections, making it easier for your students to follow along and grasp the content. Remember to incorporate a mix of text, visuals, and interactive elements to keep your students engaged throughout the course.

While writing your lesson materials, keep in mind the importance of clarity and simplicity. Use language that is easy to understand, avoiding jargon or overly complicated terminology. Present information in a logical and sequential manner, ensuring that each lesson builds upon the previous one. Additionally, include real-life examples and case studies to help students relate the concepts to their own experiences.

Building high-quality lesson materials also involves incorporating various multimedia elements. Consider using videos, audio recordings, slideshows, and infographics to enhance the learning experience. Visual aids can help clarify complex ideas and make the content more memorable. Additionally, interactive exercises and quizzes can promote active learning and reinforce key concepts.

Lastly, always strive for continuous improvement. Collect feedback from your students and use it to refine your lesson materials. Pay attention to areas that may need clarification or additional resources. By constantly evaluating and updating your course materials, you can ensure that your signature course remains relevant and valuable to your students.

By developing high-quality lesson materials is a critical step in creating a successful signature course. By conducting thorough research, planning a clear structure, using simple language, incorporating multimedia elements, and seeking feedback for improvement, you can create engaging and impactful lesson materials that will leave a lasting impression on your audience. Remember, the quality of your course materials reflects your expertise and dedication to your students' success.

Incorporating Interactive Activities and Assessments

One of the key elements to creating a successful and engaging signature course is incorporating interactive activities and assessments. These elements not only make your course more enjoyable for your students but also help them retain the information better and apply it to real-life situations. In this subchapter, we will explore some effective strategies for incorporating interactive activities and assessments into your course.

Interactive activities are a fantastic way to keep your students engaged throughout the course. Instead of just passively consuming information, they get to actively participate and interact with the content. This can be done through various methods such as group discussions, case studies, role-playing exercises, and hands-on projects. For example, if you are teaching a course on how to plan, write, and build a signature course, you can have your students collaborate in small groups to brainstorm course topics, create outlines, or even develop mini-lessons.

Assessments, on the other hand, allow you to gauge your students' understanding of the material and measure their progress. They come in different forms, such as quizzes, tests, assignments, or even self-reflection exercises. By regularly assessing your students, you can identify any gaps in their knowledge and provide additional support or clarification as needed. This will ensure that they are on track and fully comprehending the course material.

When incorporating interactive activities and assessments, it's crucial to strike a balance between challenge and accessibility. You want to provide activities and assessments that are stimulating and thought-provoking, but not so difficult that they discourage your students. Additionally, ensure that your course platform or learning management system supports interactive features and provides a seamless experience for your students.

Remember, the goal is to create an immersive learning experience that captivates your audience and helps them achieve their desired outcomes. By incorporating interactive activities and assessments, you are not only enhancing their learning journey but also increasing the value they receive from your course.

As a conclusion, incorporating interactive activities and assessments into your signature course is essential for creating an engaging and effective learning experience. By encouraging active participation and providing opportunities for assessment, you can ensure that your students are fully immersed in the content and able to apply what they have learned. So, get creative, think outside the box, and make your course an interactive and transformative experience for your entrepreneurial audience.

Chapter 5: Building Your Course Platform and Infrastructure

Choosing the Right Learning Management System (LMS)

As an entrepreneur, venturing into the world of online courses and creating your signature course can be a game-changer for your business. It allows you to share your expertise, reach a wider audience, and generate passive income. However, one crucial element that can make or break your course is the Learning Management System (LMS) you choose to deliver your content.

An LMS is a software application that enables you to create, manage, and deliver your online courses. It acts as a virtual classroom, providing a centralized hub for your course materials, interactive activities, assessments, and student progress tracking. With numerous options available in the market, selecting the right LMS for your needs can be overwhelming. Here are a few factors to consider when making this crucial decision:

1. Ease of Use: Look for an LMS that is intuitive and user-friendly, both for you as the course creator and for your students. A complicated interface can deter learners from engaging with your content and hinder your course's success.

2. Course Customization: Ensure that the LMS allows you to customize the course layout, branding, and design to reflect your unique style and brand identity. This will help create a seamless user experience and maintain consistency with your overall business aesthetic.

3. Content Delivery Options: Consider the type of content you plan to offer in your course. Does the LMS support a variety of multimedia formats, such as videos, audio files, PDFs, and quizzes? Having diverse content options will enhance the learning experience and cater to different learning preferences.

4. Payment Integration: If you intend to charge for your course, check if the LMS integrates with popular payment gateways. Streamlining the payment process will make it easier for your students to enroll and for you to receive payments seamlessly.

5. Analytics and Reporting: A robust LMS should provide detailed analytics and reporting features. This data will help you track student progress, identify areas of improvement, and refine your course content accordingly.

6. Customer Support: Look for an LMS provider that offers reliable customer support, including technical assistance and prompt responses to your queries. This will save you time and frustration, allowing you to focus on creating and delivering exceptional course content.

Remember, choosing the right LMS is a critical decision that will impact the success of your signature course. Take the time to research and evaluate different options before making a final decision. By considering factors such as ease of use, customization options, content delivery, payment integration, analytics, and customer support, you'll be well on your way to launching a highly effective and engaging online course that resonates with your target audience.

Designing an Engaging and User-Friendly Course Website

A well-designed course website is a key component in successfully launching your signature course. It serves as the central hub for all your course materials, resources, and communication with your students. In this subchapter, we will explore the essential elements of an engaging and user-friendly course website, providing you with practical tips to create a platform that will captivate your audience and enhance their learning experience.

First and foremost, your course website should have a clean and intuitive design. Keep the layout uncluttered, ensuring that important information is easily accessible. Use a consistent color scheme and font style that aligns with your brand identity, creating a cohesive visual experience for your students. Remember, simplicity is key to preventing overwhelm and allowing your content to shine.

Organize your course content in a logical manner, with clear navigation menus and intuitive pathways. Break down your course into modules and lessons, providing your students with a clear roadmap of what they can expect to learn and accomplish. Utilize clear headings, subheadings, and bullet points to make your content scannable and digestible.

Integration of multimedia elements is crucial to engage your students and make your course content more dynamic. Embed videos, audio recordings, and interactive quizzes to enhance the learning experience. Ensure that all multimedia elements are of high quality and optimized for fast loading times.

Interactivity and engagement are vital components of a successful course website. Incorporate discussion forums, chat features, and live Q&A sessions to foster a sense of community among your students. Encourage active participation and collaboration, providing opportunities for students to connect with each other and share their insights and experiences.

To make your course website user-friendly, ensure that it is mobile-responsive and accessible across different devices. Test your website on various browsers and screen sizes to guarantee optimal performance. Provide clear instructions and tutorials for navigating the website, making it easy for even the least tech-savvy students to navigate and access the course materials.

In fine, regularly update your course website with fresh content, additional resources, and improvements based on student feedback. Continuously monitor its performance, tracking metrics such as engagement, completion rates, and student satisfaction. Use this feedback to refine your website and enhance the learning experience for future students.

In sum, designing an engaging and user-friendly course website is paramount for the success of your signature course launch. By following these tips and incorporating interactive elements, organized content, and a visually appealing design, you will create a platform that captivates your audience and facilitates their learning journey. Remember, your course website is not just a platform; it is an extension of your brand and a reflection of your commitment to delivering a valuable educational experience.

Setting Up Payment Gateways and Enrollment Processes

In today's digital age, creating and launching an online course has become an increasingly popular way for entrepreneurs to share their expertise and generate passive income. However, before you can start enrolling students and receiving payments, you need to set up payment gateways and establish a smooth enrollment process. In this subchapter, we will guide you through the necessary steps to seamlessly integrate payment gateways and create an enrollment process that converts.

To begin, it's essential to select the right payment gateway for your signature course. There are numerous options available, including PayPal, Stripe, and Square, among others. Each gateway has its own advantages and fees, so it's crucial to research and choose the one that aligns best with your business needs. Once you have selected a payment gateway, you will need to create an account and integrate it into your course platform or website.

Then you'll want to design a seamless enrollment process that encourages potential students to sign up for your course. Start by creating a visually appealing and informative sales page that highlights the value and benefits of your signature course. Clearly outline the course content, learning objectives, and any bonuses or extras included. Use persuasive language and testimonials to build trust and credibility with your audience.

To incentivize enrollment, consider offering an early bird discount or a limited-time bonus for those who sign up within a specific timeframe. This creates a sense of urgency and encourages potential students to take action immediately. Additionally, make the enrollment process as straightforward and user-friendly as possible. Minimize the number of steps required and ensure that your payment gateway is easy to navigate.

Once the payment is complete, it's essential to have an automated confirmation email sent to the student, welcoming them to the course and providing any necessary login details or instructions. This not only creates a positive first impression but also reduces your workload by automating the process.

By setting up payment gateways and designing a smooth enrollment process, you are creating a seamless experience for your potential students. This subchapter has provided you with the necessary guidance to integrate payment gateways effectively and establish an enrollment process that encourages conversions. Now, you can confidently launch and monetize your signature course, knowing that your payment and enrollment systems are working flawlessly.

Chapter 6: Creating Irresistible Course Marketing Materials

Designing a Captivating Sales Page for Your Course

As an entrepreneur looking to launch your signature course, one of the most crucial elements of your marketing strategy is designing a captivating sales page. Your sales page is where potential students will come to learn about your course, understand its value, and ultimately make the decision to enroll. In this subchapter, we will explore the essential components and best practices for creating a sales page that grabs attention and converts visitors into paying students.

First and foremost, your sales page should clearly communicate the transformation and benefits that your course offers. Entrepreneurs participating in the "How to plan, write, and build your signature course in a 5-day challenge launch" niche understand the importance of delivering tangible results to their students. Highlight the specific outcomes your course will deliver and explain how it will address their pain points and challenges.

To capture your audience's attention, it's essential to have an attention-grabbing headline. Craft a headline that instantly communicates the main benefit of your course and piques curiosity. Remember, entrepreneurs are often busy individuals, so make sure your headline is concise and impactful.

When it comes to the body of your sales page, utilize persuasive copywriting techniques. Use persuasive language and storytelling to connect with your audience on an emotional level. Share success stories and testimonials from previous students to build trust and credibility. Entrepreneurs want to see that your course has worked for others in similar situations.

Incorporate visual elements such as high-quality images, videos, and infographics to break up the text and make your sales page visually appealing. Use colors, fonts, and formatting that align with your brand and create a cohesive look and feel.

Another important aspect is to include clear and compelling calls-to-action (CTAs). Use action-oriented language and make it easy for visitors to enroll in your course. Offer incentives like limited-time discounts or bonuses to create a sense of urgency.

Last but not least make your sales page easy to navigate and mobile-friendly. Entrepreneurs are often on-the-go, so ensure that your page loads quickly and is accessible on various devices.

Remember, your sales page is your opportunity to showcase the value and benefits of your signature course. By following these best practices and incorporating persuasive elements, you can create a captivating sales page that convinces entrepreneurs to enroll in your course and embark on their journey towards success.

Crafting Compelling Email Sequences for Promotion

In today's digital age, email marketing continues to be one of the most effective ways to promote your products or services. As an entrepreneur, it is crucial to master the art of crafting compelling email sequences to maximize your chances of successfully launching your signature course. In this subchapter, we will explore the strategies and techniques to plan, write, and build email sequences that captivate your audience and drive them towards taking action.

The first step in crafting a compelling email sequence is to meticulously plan your campaign. Start by identifying the goal of your promotion and the key messages you want to convey. Determine the length of your sequence, keeping in mind that it should be long enough to provide value and build anticipation, but not too long that it becomes overwhelming for your subscribers.

After that focus on writing engaging and persuasive content. Your emails should be concise, yet informative, and written in a conversational tone to establish a connection with your readers. Begin your sequence with a captivating subject line that grabs attention and entices recipients to open the email. Personalize your emails by addressing subscribers by their names, and use storytelling techniques to make the content relatable and memorable.

To build anticipation and maintain your audience's interest, consider using a series of email templates. These templates can be customized to suit your unique brand voice and provide consistency throughout your sequence. Make sure to incorporate a clear call to action in each email, guiding your subscribers towards the desired action, whether it be signing up for a webinar, purchasing your course, or joining a waitlist.

In addition to well-crafted content, it's important to optimize your email sequences for deliverability and engagement. Pay attention to your email deliverability rates by ensuring your emails are not marked as spam. Use an email marketing platform that provides analytics and tracking features to monitor open and click-through rates, allowing you to refine your strategies based on real-time data.

All in all, crafting compelling email sequences for promotion is an essential skill for entrepreneurs looking to successfully launch their signature courses. By carefully planning, writing captivating content, and optimizing for deliverability and engagement, you can create email sequences that capture your audience's attention, build anticipation, and ultimately drive them towards taking action. With practice and refinement, you can master the art of email marketing and propel your business to new heights.

Utilizing Social Media and Content Marketing Strategies

In today's digital age, social media and content marketing have become indispensable tools for entrepreneurs looking to launch their signature courses successfully. With billions of active users across various platforms, social media provides a vast opportunity to reach and engage with your target audience. Coupled with effective content marketing strategies, you can create a buzz around your course and attract a significant number of participants in just five days.

1. Develop a social media plan: Before diving into the world of social media, it's crucial to develop a plan that aligns with your course launch objectives. Identify the platforms where your target audience is most active and create a content calendar to schedule posts. This plan will help you stay organized and maintain consistency throughout the launch period.

2. Engage and interact with your audience: Social media is all about building connections. Engage with your audience by responding to comments, asking questions, and encouraging discussions related to your course topic. This interaction not only builds trust but also increases the chances of participants spreading the word about your course.

3. Leverage user-generated content: Encourage your audience to share their experiences, testimonials, or progress related to your course. User-generated content acts as social proof and can influence others to join. Share these posts on your social media channels and tag the participants to show appreciation and encourage further engagement.

4. Create compelling content: Content marketing is a powerful tool to attract and retain your target audience. Craft informative blog posts, videos, or podcasts that provide value to your audience and establish you as an expert in your niche. Share these pieces consistently on your social media platforms to keep your audience engaged and interested in your course.

5. Collaborate with influencers and affiliates: Identify influencers or individuals in your industry with a significant following and collaborate with them to promote your course. Offer them a free enrollment or an affiliate commission for every participant they refer. Their endorsement can significantly boost your course visibility and credibility.

6. Utilize live videos and webinars: Live videos and webinars allow you to connect with your audience in real-time, answer their questions, and provide a glimpse into your course content.

Promote these events on social media, and offer exclusive bonuses or discounts to those who attend.

By leveraging social media and implementing effective content marketing strategies, you can build anticipation, engage your target audience, and attract participants to your signature course in just five days. Remember to monitor your progress, analyze the impact of your efforts, and make necessary adjustments to ensure a successful launch.

Chapter 7: Launching Your Signature Course

Preparing for Your 5-day Challenge Launch

Launching your signature course through a 5-day challenge can be an effective strategy to engage your audience, build anticipation, and generate excitement for your offer. In this subchapter, we will discuss the key steps you need to take to prepare for a successful 5-day challenge launch.

1. Define Your Goals: Before diving into the launch process, it's essential to clearly define your goals. What do you want to achieve with this challenge? Is it to generate leads, increase your authority in the industry, or drive sales for your signature course? Knowing your objectives will help you create a focused and targeted launch plan.

2. Plan Your Content: Developing a comprehensive content plan is crucial for a successful 5-day challenge launch. Outline the topics you will cover each day, ensuring they align with the transformation your course offers. Break down each day's content into smaller subtopics, making it easier for participants to digest and engage with. Additionally, consider incorporating various content formats such as videos, worksheets, and live Q&A sessions to keep your audience engaged.

3. Build Your Challenge Funnel: A well-designed challenge funnel will guide your audience from the initial opt-in to eventually enrolling in your signature course. Create an engaging landing page that clearly communicates the value of your challenge and entices visitors to sign up. Develop a series of follow-up emails to nurture your leads throughout the challenge and provide additional value. Lastly, create a sales page for your signature course that highlights its benefits and encourages participants to take the next step.

4. Promote Your Challenge: To attract participants to your 5-day challenge, you need to promote it effectively. Leverage different marketing channels, such as social media, email newsletters, and collaborations with influencers or industry partners. Craft compelling copy and visuals to grab attention and clearly communicate the benefits of joining your challenge.

5. Prepare for Engagement: As participants join your challenge, it's crucial to be prepared to engage with them actively. Create a dedicated Facebook group or online community where participants can connect, ask questions, and share their progress. Be present and provide valuable insights, answering questions promptly and fostering a supportive environment.

6. Test and Optimize: As you launch your 5-day challenge, continuously monitor and analyze your results. Track metrics such as sign-up rates, engagement levels, and conversion rates to identify areas for improvement. Analyze participant feedback to understand their needs better and make necessary adjustments to enhance future launches.

By following these steps, you will be well-prepared to launch your signature course through a 5-day challenge successfully. Remember to stay focused, provide value, and engage with your audience throughout the process. Good luck with your challenge launch and the growth of your signature course!

Building Anticipation and Generating Buzz for Your Course

In the fast-paced world of online entrepreneurship, it's crucial to make a strong impact and stand out from the crowd. One effective way to do this is by building anticipation and generating buzz for your signature course. By creating excitement and curiosity around your offering, you can attract a larger audience and increase your chances of success. In this subchapter, we will explore various strategies to help you build anticipation and generate buzz for your course during a 5-day challenge launch.

Firstly, it's important to establish a clear timeline for your course launch. By setting specific dates for various pre-launch activities, such as teaser content, enrollment opening, and early bird discounts, you create a sense of urgency and encourage potential customers to take action. Make sure to communicate these dates to your audience in advance and create a countdown to build excitement.

Next, leverage the power of social media to create a buzz around your course. Craft compelling and shareable content that highlights the unique value and benefits of your course. Utilize platforms such as Facebook, Instagram, and LinkedIn to engage with your audience, share sneak peeks, and encourage them to spread the word. Consider hosting live Q&A sessions or sharing testimonials from previous participants to generate social proof and credibility.

Another effective strategy is to collaborate with influencers or industry experts in your niche. Their endorsement can significantly boost your course's credibility and reach. Reach out to relevant influencers and offer them a complimentary access to your course in exchange for their honest review or testimonial. Additionally, consider hosting joint webinars or guest blogging on their platforms to tap into their existing audience and generate buzz.

Creating a sense of exclusivity can also fuel anticipation and generate buzz. Consider offering limited spots or early-bird discounts to your course, creating a fear of missing out (FOMO) among your audience. By emphasizing the scarcity of your offering, you can create a sense of urgency and motivate potential customers to take action.

Finally utilize email marketing to your advantage. Craft persuasive email sequences that tease the valuable content your course offers. Offer free resources or mini-lessons as lead magnets to entice your audience to sign up for your mailing list. Send regular updates and reminders leading up to the launch to keep the excitement alive.

Building anticipation and generating buzz for your signature course is a critical step in ensuring a successful launch. By implementing these strategies, you can engage your audience, create a sense of excitement, and increase your chances of attracting a large number of participants. Stay consistent, leverage various marketing channels, and keep your audience engaged throughout the process.

Executing an Effective Launch Strategy

Launching a signature course is an exciting endeavor for entrepreneurs looking to monetize their expertise and share their knowledge with a wider audience. However, without a well-executed launch strategy, even the most valuable course can fall flat. In this subchapter, we will explore the key steps to executing an effective launch strategy for your signature course within the timeframe of a 5-day challenge.

1. Define Your Launch Goals: Before diving into the execution phase, it is crucial to define clear and measurable goals for your course launch. Are you aiming for a certain number of sign-ups, revenue targets, or audience engagement? By setting specific goals, you can tailor your launch strategy accordingly and have a benchmark for success.

2. Pre-Launch Buzz: Building anticipation and excitement before your course launch is essential. Engage with your audience through social media, email newsletters, or even live webinars to create a buzz around your upcoming challenge. Tease the benefits and outcomes of your course while offering valuable content to showcase your expertise.

3. Craft a Compelling Sales Page: Your sales page will be the primary point of conversion for potential customers. It should clearly communicate the value of your course, addressing pain points and highlighting the transformation participants will experience. Utilize persuasive copywriting techniques, testimonials, and attention-grabbing visuals to compel visitors to take action.

4. Leverage Strategic Partnerships: Collaborating with influencers or complementary businesses can significantly amplify your reach and credibility. Consider partnering with relevant industry leaders who can promote your course to their audience. Additionally, guest blogging or podcast interviews can help you establish yourself as an authority in your niche.

5. Implement a Deadline-Driven Enrollment Period: Creating a sense of urgency and scarcity can drive more sign-ups. Implement a limited-time enrollment period, accompanied by a countdown timer, to motivate potential customers to take action. Offering early-bird discounts or exclusive bonuses for those who enroll during the challenge can further incentivize participation.

6. Engage and Nurture Your Audience: During the 5-day challenge, it is crucial to maintain regular communication with your audience. Provide valuable content, answer questions promptly, and offer support to ensure a positive participant experience. Building rapport and trust will increase the likelihood of course enrollment and future referrals.

7. Follow-Up and Retention Strategies: After the challenge ends, continue nurturing your participants. Offer additional resources or exclusive community access to keep them engaged. Implement post-launch surveys to gather feedback and testimonials, which can be used for future marketing efforts.

Executing an effective launch strategy requires careful planning, consistent communication, and a deep understanding of your target audience's needs. By following these steps, you can create a successful launch for your signature course within a 5-day challenge, setting the stage for long-term success as an entrepreneur in the world of online education.

Chapter 8: Engaging with Your Course Participants

Building a Supportive Community for Your Course

One of the key factors in the success of your signature course is the community you build around it. A supportive community not only enhances the learning experience for your students but also helps you establish yourself as an authority in your niche. In this subchapter, we will discuss strategies for creating and nurturing a strong and engaged community for your course.

First and foremost, it is important to lay a solid foundation for your community. Start by clearly defining the purpose and values of your course. What is the ultimate goal you want your students to achieve? What kind of environment do you want to create? Communicate this vision to your audience and let them know what to expect when they join your course.

Next, consider the platforms you will use to host your community. There are various options available, including private Facebook groups, online forums, or dedicated course platforms. Choose a platform that aligns with your goals and makes it easy for your students to interact with each other and with you as the instructor.

Once your community is set up, focus on fostering engagement. Encourage students to introduce themselves and share their goals and expectations for the course. Regularly post relevant and valuable content to spark discussions and provide insights. Be present and actively participate in these discussions to build rapport with your students and address any questions or concerns they may have.

To further encourage community engagement, consider incorporating interactive elements into your course. This could include live Q&A sessions, group projects, or peer-to-peer feedback sessions. These activities not only facilitate learning but also foster collaboration and a sense of belonging within the community.

In addition to active participation, it is crucial to create a safe and supportive environment for your students. Set clear guidelines for respectful communication and intervene if any conflicts arise. Encourage students to support and uplift each other, fostering a sense of camaraderie within the community.

Lastly, continuously evaluate and improve your community-building efforts. Seek feedback from your students and implement changes accordingly. Regularly assess the effectiveness of your chosen platform and make adjustments if necessary. By constantly refining your community-building strategies, you can ensure a thriving and supportive environment for your course.

In conclusion, building a supportive community is essential for the success of your signature course. By laying a solid foundation, fostering engagement, creating a safe environment, and continuously improving your efforts, you can cultivate a thriving community that enhances the learning experience for your students and establishes you as an authority in your niche.

Encouraging Active Participation and Discussion

One of the key elements to a successful signature course is active participation and discussion among your students. As an entrepreneur, it is crucial to foster an engaging and interactive learning environment that encourages students to actively participate in the course material and discussions. In this subchapter, we will explore various strategies to promote active participation and discussion within your signature course.

1. Set clear expectations: From the very beginning, communicate to your students the importance of active participation and discussion. Let them know that their input and engagement are not only welcomed but also crucial for their own learning experience.

2. Create a safe and supportive environment: Build a community where students feel comfortable sharing their thoughts and ideas.

Encourage respect and open-mindedness, emphasizing that all opinions are valued. Foster a sense of community by creating discussion forums or social media groups where students can connect and interact with each other.

3. Use interactive teaching methods:
Incorporate diverse teaching methods to cater to different learning styles. Utilize videos, quizzes, case studies, and group activities to keep the course material engaging and promote active participation. Consider including live webinars or Q&A sessions, where students can interact with you directly and ask questions.

4. Assign group projects or discussions: Divide
students into smaller groups and assign them group projects or discussion topics related to the course material. This not only encourages active participation but also fosters collaboration and peer-to-peer learning. Encourage group members to share their findings or insights with the entire class.

5. Provide regular feedback and encouragement: Give students timely feedback on their participation, contributions, and assignments. Acknowledge and appreciate their efforts to keep them motivated. Offer constructive criticism when necessary, but always in a supportive manner. Celebrate their achievements and encourage them to continue actively participating.

6. Lead by example: As the course creator, actively participate in discussions, provide prompt responses to questions, and engage with students' ideas. By leading the way, you set a positive example for your students and encourage them to follow suit.

By implementing these strategies, you can create a dynamic and engaging learning environment that encourages active participation and discussion among your students. Remember, the more engaged and involved your students are, the more they will gain from your signature course, leading to higher satisfaction rates and increased success for both you and your students.

Providing Ongoing Support and Feedback

As an entrepreneur, creating and launching your signature course is just the first step towards success. To ensure the long-term growth and sustainability of your course, it is crucial to provide ongoing support and feedback to your students. This subchapter will guide you on how to effectively deliver continuous assistance and valuable feedback to your course participants.

One of the most important aspects of providing ongoing support is creating a community for your students. By establishing a platform such as a private Facebook group or an online forum, you can facilitate interaction and collaboration among your students. Encourage them to ask questions, share their progress, and connect with one another. This community will not only provide a sense of belonging but also foster peer-to-peer learning and support.

Another crucial aspect of ongoing support is offering regular check-ins and accountability mechanisms. Set up weekly or monthly live Q&A sessions where students can address their concerns and receive personalized feedback. Additionally, consider assigning accountability partners or creating accountability groups to help students stay on track and motivate each other throughout the course.

Feedback is a powerful tool for growth and improvement. Incorporate feedback loops into your course structure to continuously enhance the learning experience. Provide opportunities for students to give feedback on the content, delivery, and overall experience of the course. This feedback can be collected through surveys, polls, or even one-on-one conversations. Actively listen to your students' suggestions and incorporate necessary changes to refine your course and meet their needs better.

Furthermore, consider offering additional resources and bonuses to enhance the learning journey. This could include supplementary materials, expert interviews, or exclusive access to relevant tools and software. By continually adding value to your course, you will strengthen the bond with your students and increase their satisfaction and chances of success.

Remember, providing ongoing support and feedback is not only beneficial for your students but also for your business. Satisfied students are more likely to become repeat customers and advocates for your course. Their success stories and testimonials will attract new participants and contribute to the growth of your course.

In general, by establishing a supportive community, offering regular check-ins, incorporating feedback loops, and providing valuable resources, you can ensure the long-term success of your signature course. Remember, the journey does not end with the course launch; it is an ongoing process of nurturing and supporting your students' growth.

Chapter 9: Measuring and Improving Course Success

Analyzing Course Metrics and Feedback

As an entrepreneur looking to create and launch your own signature course, it's crucial to understand the importance of analyzing course metrics and feedback. By diving into the data and listening to your audience, you can gain valuable insights that will help you refine and improve your course content, delivery, and overall student experience.

One of the first steps in analyzing course metrics is to track student engagement and completion rates. This data will give you an understanding of how your audience is interacting with your course materials and whether they are completing the entire course or dropping off at certain points. By identifying any areas of low engagement, you can make necessary adjustments to keep your students motivated and engaged throughout the entire course.

Additionally, monitoring the feedback and comments from your students is crucial. This feedback can provide you with valuable insights into what is working well and what needs improvement within your course. Pay attention to common themes or issues that arise and take the necessary steps to address them. By actively listening to your students and making improvements based on their feedback, you can create a course that meets their needs and exceeds their expectations.

Furthermore, analyzing course metrics can also help you identify any technical or logistical issues that may be hindering the student experience. For example, if you notice a high drop-off rate during a specific video lesson, it could be an indication that the video quality is poor or the content is not resonating with your audience. By identifying and resolving these issues, you can enhance the overall learning experience for your students.

In addition to analyzing course metrics, it's also important to gather testimonials and success stories from your students. These testimonials can be powerful marketing tools that showcase the value and effectiveness of your course. They can also provide you with insights into the specific aspects of your course that resonate most with your audience.

Analyzing course metrics and feedback is an essential part of creating and launching a successful signature course. By paying close attention to student engagement, feedback, and testimonials, you can continuously improve your course and create an exceptional learning experience for your students. Remember, the success of your course ultimately lies in the hands of your students, so make sure to listen and adapt accordingly.

Identifying Areas for Improvement and Expansion

As an entrepreneur, constantly seeking ways to improve and expand your business is crucial for long term success. In the subchapter on "Identifying Areas for Improvement and Expansion" from the book "Launch Your Signature Course in 5 Days: A Step-by-Step Guide for Entrepreneurs," we will delve into the key strategies and techniques you can employ to take your course to the next level.

When planning, writing, and building your signature course in a 5-day challenge launch, it is essential to keep a keen eye on areas where you can enhance the value you offer and explore opportunities for growth. Here are some valuable insights to help you identify areas for improvement and expansion:

1. **Analyzing Feedback:** Actively seek feedback from your course participants through surveys, interviews, or testimonials. Identifying common themes and suggestions will provide valuable insights into areas you can improve upon.

2. **Monitoring Course Metrics:** Track important metrics such as completion rates, engagement levels, and satisfaction scores. These metrics can highlight areas where participants struggle or lose interest, allowing you to refine your content and delivery accordingly.

3. Staying Updated with Industry Trends:
Continuously research and stay up-to-date with the latest trends and advancements in your niche. This will enable you to identify gaps in your course content and explore opportunities for expansion.

4. Leveraging Technology: Embrace technology tools and platforms that can enhance the learning experience for your participants. Utilize interactive elements, gamification, or multimedia to make your course more engaging and impactful.

5. Seeking Collaboration and Partnerships:
Identify potential collaborations and partnerships within your industry. Collaborating with experts or complementary businesses can provide opportunities for joint ventures, guest lectures, or additional resources to further enrich your course.

6. Segmenting and Personalizing Content:
Analyze your audience and consider segmenting your course content to cater to specific needs or skill levels. Personalizing the learning experience will enhance participant satisfaction and attract a wider range of learners.

7. Exploring New Formats or Delivery Methods:
Consider offering your course in different formats
or delivery methods such as live webinars, self-
paced modules, or group coaching sessions.
Experimenting with new approaches can attract a
broader audience and expand your reach.

By consistently identifying areas for improvement
and expansion, you will not only enhance the quality
of your signature course but also stay ahead of the
competition in your niche. Remember, growth and
evolution are vital for long-term success as an
entrepreneur. So, take the time to analyze,
innovate, and adapt your course to meet the ever-
changing needs of your audience.

Iterating and Enhancing Your Signature Course Over Time

As an entrepreneur, creating a signature course is
an excellent way to showcase your expertise,
establish your authority, and generate passive
income. However, the work doesn't end once you've
launched your course. In fact, it's just the
beginning. To ensure the long-term success of your

signature course, you need to continually iterate and enhance it over time. In this subchapter, we will explore the strategies and techniques that will help you refine and improve your course as you go along.

One of the first steps in iterating your signature course is to gather feedback from your students. This can be done through surveys, testimonials, or even one-on-one conversations. By understanding the strengths and weaknesses of your course, you can make informed decisions on what areas to enhance. Take note of the common pain points or areas of confusion and work towards resolving them.

Another way to enhance your course is by staying up-to-date with the latest industry trends and developments. As an entrepreneur, it's important to keep evolving with the changing landscape. Incorporate new insights, research, or case studies that are relevant to your course material. By doing so, you can ensure your course remains valuable and competitive.

Don't be afraid to experiment and try new things. Your signature course doesn't have to remain static. Consider adding new modules, bonus content, or even guest experts to provide a fresh perspective. This not only adds value for your existing students but also attracts new ones who may be interested in the updated material.

Regularly assessing your course metrics is essential in identifying areas for improvement. Analyze the completion rates, engagement, and feedback from your students. Are there any sections that are consistently being skipped? Is there a particular topic that generates the most engagement? By understanding these patterns, you can optimize your course content for maximum impact.

Lastly, consider repurposing your course material across different formats. Some students may prefer video lessons, while others may prefer written content or audio recordings. By diversifying your course delivery methods, you can cater to different learning styles and attract a wider audience.

Launching your signature course is just the beginning of a journey. To ensure its long-term success, you need to continuously iterate and enhance your course. By gathering feedback, staying up-to-date with industry trends, experimenting with new ideas, analyzing metrics, and repurposing content, you can create a course that delivers exceptional value to your students while also growing your business. Keep refining and improving, and your signature course will become a valuable asset that sets you apart in your niche.

Chapter 10: Scaling and Monetizing Your Signature Course

Scaling Your Course to Reach a Larger Audience

Once you have successfully planned, written, and built your signature course, the next step is to find ways to reach a larger audience. Scaling your course is crucial for entrepreneurs who aim to make a significant impact and generate sustainable revenue from their expertise. By implementing the right strategies, you can expand your reach and attract more students to your program. Here are some essential steps to help you scale your course and reach a larger audience.

1. Leverage Social Media: Social media platforms such as Facebook, Instagram, and LinkedIn offer powerful tools for promoting your course. Create engaging content related to your course topic, build a strong online presence, and use targeted advertising to reach your ideal audience. Engage with your audience regularly, respond to their queries, and provide valuable insights to establish yourself as an authority in your niche.

2. Collaborate with Influencers: Identify influencers in your industry who have a large following and align with your course topic. Collaborating with influencers can greatly expand your reach and credibility. Offer them a complimentary access to your course in exchange for promoting it to their audience. This way, you can tap into their established fan base and attract new students.

3. Offer Affiliate Programs: Create an affiliate program where past students or industry professionals can earn a commission for each referral they bring to your course. This incentivizes others to promote your course and can significantly increase your reach. Provide your affiliates with promotional materials and track their progress using affiliate tracking software.

4. Repurpose Content: Repurposing your course content into different formats can help you reach a wider audience. Consider creating blog posts, podcasts, YouTube videos, or even a book based on the knowledge you've shared in your course. Adapt the content to suit different platforms and share it across multiple channels to attract new students.

5. Host Webinars and Workshops: Conduct live webinars and workshops where you can showcase the value and benefits of your course. Offer attendees a sneak peek into your course content and engage with them in real-time. Webinars provide an excellent opportunity to connect with potential students and address any doubts or concerns they may have.

Scaling your course to reach a larger audience requires strategic planning and consistent effort. By leveraging social media, collaborating with influencers, offering affiliate programs, repurposing content, and hosting webinars, you can expand your reach and attract more students to your signature course. Remember, the key is to continuously engage with your audience, provide value, and establish yourself as a trusted authority in your niche.

Exploring Additional Income Streams from Your Course

As an entrepreneur, creating and launching your signature course can be a game-changer for your business. It allows you to share your expertise, build your authority, and generate passive income. However, did you know that your course can also serve as a foundation for additional income streams? In this subchapter, we will explore some exciting possibilities to maximize your revenue potential.

One way to generate additional income from your course is by offering upsells and upgrades. Once your students have enrolled in your course, you can provide them with the option to upgrade to a higher-tier program or purchase additional resources, such as exclusive content, coaching sessions, or downloadable materials. This not only adds value to their learning experience but also increases your revenue per customer.

Another avenue to explore is affiliate partnerships. Identify complementary products or services that align with your course content, and establish partnerships with their creators or companies. By promoting these offerings to your students, you can earn a commission for each referral or sale made through your affiliate links. This not only diversifies your income but also strengthens your network within your niche.

Consider packaging your course into a membership site. This allows you to create a recurring revenue stream by charging a monthly or annual fee for continued access to your course material, updates, and exclusive community support. By providing ongoing value, you can retain your students for longer periods and generate consistent income.

Additionally, you can explore the possibility of turning your course content into a physical product. Consider creating workbooks, guidebooks, or even a printed version of your course materials. This opens up opportunities for selling physical products alongside your digital offerings, catering to different preferences and increasing your revenue streams.

Explore the potential of licensing or franchising your course. If your signature course is highly successful and sought-after, you may consider partnering with other entrepreneurs or businesses who wish to offer your course under their brand. This allows you to expand your reach, leverage their networks, and earn licensing fees or royalties.

Your signature course is not just a one-time income generator but a foundation for multiple revenue streams. By implementing upsells, affiliate partnerships, membership sites, physical products, and licensing opportunities, you can maximize your income potential and create a sustainable business model. Keep exploring and experimenting with different strategies to find the right combination that works for you and your audience.

Leveraging Your Course Success for Future Ventures

Congratulations! You have successfully planned, written, and built your signature course in just five days. You are now equipped with a powerful tool to share your expertise, grow your brand, and generate income. But your journey doesn't end here - it's time to leverage your course success for future ventures.

As an entrepreneur, you understand the importance of continually evolving and expanding your business. Your signature course is not only a valuable asset in itself but also a stepping stone towards other exciting opportunities. Here are some strategies to help you make the most of your course and propel your entrepreneurial journey forward.

1. Repurpose your course content: Your signature course is a goldmine of valuable information. Consider repackaging and repurposing the content into other formats such as ebooks, podcasts, webinars, or even one-on-one coaching sessions. This allows you to reach new audiences and monetize your expertise in different ways.

2. Create a membership or subscription model: If your course offers ongoing value, consider transforming it into a membership or subscription-based model. This not only provides a consistent stream of income but also fosters a community of loyal customers who are eager to learn from you and engage with your brand.

3. Collaborate with other experts: Seek opportunities to collaborate with other experts in your niche. You can host joint webinars, create co-authored content, or even develop a bundle of courses with complementary topics. By tapping into each other's networks, you can expand your reach and establish yourself as a thought leader within your industry.

4. Offer advanced or specialized courses: Once your audience has completed your signature course, they may be hungry for more in-depth knowledge or specialized training. Develop advanced or specialized courses that build upon the foundation you've already established. This not only provides additional value to your existing customers but also attracts new ones who are looking for advanced learning opportunities.

5. Use testimonials and success stories: Leverage the success stories and testimonials from your course participants to build credibility and attract new customers. Testimonials act as social proof and validate the effectiveness of your course. Share these testimonials on your website, social media platforms, and in your marketing materials to increase your course's visibility and generate interest.

Remember, your signature course is just the beginning of your entrepreneurial journey. By leveraging your course success, repurposing content, exploring new models, collaborating with others, and providing advanced courses, you can continue to grow your brand, expand your reach, and generate income in exciting new ways. Embrace the possibilities, stay innovative, and continue to make a difference through your expertise.

Chapter 11: Conclusion and Next Steps

Celebrating Your Course Launch Accomplishments

Congratulations, entrepreneurs! You have successfully completed the 5-day challenge and are now ready to celebrate your course launch accomplishments. This subchapter is all about recognizing your hard work, reflecting on your journey, and embracing the exciting possibilities that lie ahead.

Launching a signature course is no small feat. It requires meticulous planning, dedicated writing, and building a course that truly delivers value to your audience. Throughout the process, you have pushed through obstacles, honed your expertise, and created something incredible.

Now is the time to give yourself a well-deserved pat on the back. Celebrating your course launch accomplishments not only acknowledges your hard work but also boosts your confidence and motivation for future endeavors. So, let's dive into some ideas on how you can celebrate this exciting milestone:

1. Toast to Your Success: Gather your team, loved ones, or fellow entrepreneurs who supported you during this journey and raise a glass to your achievement. Share stories, laughter, and express gratitude for the collective effort that made your course launch possible.

2. Reflect on Your Journey: Take a moment to look back and appreciate how far you've come. Reflect on the challenges you overcame, the skills you developed, and the growth you experienced. Celebrate the lessons learned and acknowledge your dedication and perseverance.

3. Share Your Success with Your Audience: Engage with your audience and let them share in your excitement. Send a heartfelt email expressing gratitude for their support and offer them exclusive discounts or bonuses to celebrate the launch together. Consider hosting a live Q&A session or a virtual party to interact with your audience and answer any questions they may have.

4. Treat Yourself: You've worked tirelessly to create an exceptional course, so why not treat yourself to something special? Whether it's a spa day, a weekend getaway, or a fancy dinner, indulge in a well-deserved reward to recharge and rejuvenate.

5. Set New Goals: Celebrating your course launch accomplishments is just the beginning. Use this milestone as a stepping stone towards even greater achievements. Set new goals for your course, plan for future launches, and continue to refine your expertise.

Remember, celebrating your course launch accomplishments is not just about reveling in the present moment, but also about setting the stage for your future success. Take this time to acknowledge your hard work, appreciate your supporters, and embrace the exciting possibilities that lie ahead. You have the power to make a significant impact in the lives of your audience, and this is just the beginning of an incredible journey. Cheers to your success!

Reflecting on Lessons Learned and Successes Achieved

As entrepreneurs, we are constantly learning and evolving, gathering new insights and experiences along the way. Our journey to launch a signature course is no different. In this subchapter, we take a moment to reflect on the lessons learned and successes achieved during our 5-day challenge launch.

The first lesson learned is the power of planning. In order to successfully launch a signature course in just five days, meticulous planning is essential. We discovered that setting clear objectives, outlining the course structure, and creating a timeline were crucial steps in ensuring a smooth and efficient launch. By investing time in the planning phase, we were able to streamline the process and avoid unnecessary setbacks.

Another valuable lesson we learned was the importance of effective writing. A signature course requires compelling content that engages and educates the audience. Through this 5-day challenge launch, we honed our writing skills, focusing on clarity, conciseness, and authenticity. We discovered that by communicating our message effectively, we were able to establish a genuine connection with our audience, earning their trust and loyalty.

Building a signature course within such a tight timeframe also taught us the power of prioritization and focus. We realized the need to identify the core elements of our course and allocate our time and resources accordingly. By staying focused on the most critical aspects, we were able to create a high-quality course that resonated with our target audience, while still meeting our tight deadline.

Reflecting on our successes, we celebrated the milestones achieved during the 5-day challenge launch. From the initial idea conception to the final launch, we witnessed the transformation of our vision into a tangible reality. We saw firsthand the impact our signature course had on our audience, as they gained valuable knowledge and skills that empowered them on their own entrepreneurial journeys.

Finally, we learned the importance of adaptability and flexibility. Launching a signature course within a short timeframe requires the ability to adapt to unforeseen obstacles and adjust our strategies accordingly. We discovered that being open to feedback, continuously refining our approach, and embracing change were key elements in our success.

Reflecting on the lessons learned and successes achieved during our 5-day challenge launch has been an invaluable exercise for us as entrepreneurs. We have gained insights into the power of planning, effective writing, prioritization, focus, adaptability, and flexibility. Armed with this knowledge, we are ready to embark on future endeavors with confidence, knowing that we have the tools and strategies to launch our signature courses successfully.

Outlining Your Next Steps for Course Evolution and Growth

Congratulations on completing the 5-day challenge and successfully launching your signature course! Now that your course is out in the world, it's time to think about its evolution and growth. In this subchapter, we will discuss the crucial steps you need to take to ensure the continuous development and success of your course.

1. Reflect on Your Launch: Take a moment to evaluate the results of your course launch. What worked well, and what could be improved? Analyzing your launch will provide valuable insights that will guide your next steps. Consider gathering feedback from participants to gain a deeper understanding of their experience.

2. Assess Course Performance: Dive into the analytics and metrics of your course to gauge its performance. How many students enrolled? How many completed the course? What was the average completion rate? Analyzing these numbers will help you identify areas for improvement and opportunities for growth.

3. Update and Enhance Content: Based on the feedback and performance assessment, make necessary updates and enhancements to your course content. Look for ways to improve clarity, add more value, and address any gaps or areas of confusion. Remember, a course that constantly evolves and stays relevant will attract new students and keep existing ones engaged.

4. Expand Your Audience: Consider ways to reach a broader audience. Explore marketing strategies, such as social media advertising, collaborations, or partnerships with influencers in your niche. Additionally, optimize your website and landing pages to improve search engine visibility and attract organic traffic.

5. Offer Advanced Modules or Upsells: Once your course gains popularity, you can create advanced modules or additional resources that provide further value to your students. This not only helps you generate additional revenue but also deepens the learning experience and establishes you as an expert in your field.

6. Engage with Your Community: Building a strong community around your course is essential for its growth. Encourage students to interact with each other through discussion forums, live Q&A sessions, or private Facebook groups. Actively participate in these conversations, provide support, and foster a sense of belonging.

7. Continual Learning and Professional Development: As an entrepreneur, it's crucial to stay updated with the latest industry trends and best practices. Invest in your own learning and professional development to ensure your course remains cutting-edge and valuable for your audience.

Launching your signature course is just the beginning of an exciting journey. By outlining your next steps for course evolution and growth, you are setting yourself up for continued success. Embrace feedback, adapt to changes, and always strive to provide exceptional value to your students. Remember, a thriving course is a result

of constant evolution and a commitment to
excellence.

www.ingramcontent.com/pod-product-compliance
Lightning Source LLC
Chambersburg PA
CBHW062333290526
45794CB00005B/2013